# Why I Believe in Ghosts

*poems by*

# Neil Grill

*Finishing Line Press*
Georgetown, Kentucky

# Why I Believe in Ghosts

*To my parents, Belle and Leon Grill,
in memory, and with love*

Copyright © 2021 by Neil Grill
ISBN 978-1-64662-396-9  First Edition

All rights reserved under International and Pan-American Copyright Conventions. No part of this book may be reproduced in any manner whatsoever without written permission from the publisher, except in the case of brief quotations embodied in critical articles and reviews.

## ACKNOWLEDGMENTS

'Illuminations' poems, 2019, 92nd Street Y Himan Brown Senior Program

Compound Words
If I Can't be an Angel
Mephistos

Publisher: Leah Huete de Maines
Editor: Christen Kincaid
Cover Art: Genese Grill
Author Photo: Judith Smith
Cover Design: Alessandro Segalini

Order online: www.finishinglinepress.com
also available on amazon.com

Author inquiries and mail orders:
Finishing Line Press
PO Box 1626
Georgetown, Kentucky 40324
USA

# Table of Contents

I Wrote a Villanelle Thirty Years Ago ................................................... 1

The Child Asked, 'Don't You Like Me Anymore?' ............................. 2

Why I Believe in Ghosts ....................................................................... 5

Half Sestina on My Mother's Centenary ............................................ 8

Coupons.................................................................................................. 9

Company Fruit..................................................................................... 12

Compound Words............................................................................... 13

I Wish My Father Had Told Me........................................................ 15

'I am doing things I haven't done before' ........................................ 16

Perilous: June 1986.............................................................................. 17

Nyack, N.Y. Winter Morning 1988.................................................... 18

Silent Watchman.................................................................................. 19

Mt. Sinai December 2016 ................................................................... 21

I Don't Give a Damn about Revision ............................................... 25

I'm Waiting for the Poem to Write Itself ......................................... 27

Found and Made Poem...................................................................... 28

'One More Song He Had'................................................................... 30

Still Life ................................................................................................. 31

If I Can't Be an Angel ......................................................................... 32

Mephistos ............................................................................................. 33

## I Wrote a Villanelle Thirty Years Ago

I wrote a villanelle thirty years ago.
About a girl in a red autumn coat.
I never wrote another poem again.

It's on a shelf in my clothes closet
in a worn, leather briefcase with a clasp.
I wrote that poem thirty years ago.

It's in a blue binder with my other poems.
A manuscript I never published.
I never wrote a poem again.

I've carried that briefcase, poems, from
house to house, marriage to marriage.
I wrote a villanelle thirty years ago.

My life cracked in half thirty years ago.
Say it was about a girl in a red autumn coat.
I never wrote a poem again.

Until just now. I start again.
Unclasp my heart, my leather voice.
I wrote a villanelle thirty years ago.
I write another one today.

## The Child Asked, 'Don't you like me anymore?'

*For Philip Bromberg*[1]

The child asked, 'Don't you like me anymore?'
And I didn't know how to answer. Like the guy
waving his unlit cigar at me all the way to the
airport, that day forty years ago, calling me, 'Son,'
though he was scarcely five years older than me.
'Son, one thing I learned all my years on the road,
when you're out of New York, you're out-a-town.'
As far as the child and me, I'd been out-a-town,
or maybe in and out, swearing I'd be back,
never staying long, door closing behind me.

The child knew what he had come here for,
here, this earth, this Bronx, three months before Hitler invaded Poland.
He knew, sparse as he was, four pounds, he had enough to survive,
knew because he had been told,
some wordless telepathy, vouchsafed to him.

But I was reading from the book of mixed messages,
like even Western Union closed up shop, and
though I didn't abuse the child, neglect closer to the truth,
yo, they're both the same, when you come down to it.

Child asked me, 'Don't you like me anymore?',
even when I told him, 'Look, there'll be time, I won't forget you'.
And didn't it take courage to buck my father at 19,
stopping at half-way houses, travelling ten years carrying
Defoe, Dickens $1.45 Modern Libraries in my rucksack.
Didn't you hear him call me, 'Quitter, good for a girl!'
Didn't I promise I'd come and get you;
we'd have real time together, just you and me.
And didn't I keep that promise, at least for a while,
you and me hanging out,
readings, workshops, and all those poems we composed together,
three, four an issue, the 'Littles,' *Windsor Review, Pivot.*

Yeah, I know, I know,
I left you in the kitchen with the electric typewriter,
Rachmaninoff on the record player, summer trees bursting outside,
to go off with the thin woman with green eyes, she on top of me,
saying, 'Not yet, not yet,' and I could have helped myself if I could,
but I couldn't, and when it ended, flesh to ashes,
surviving on once-chewed prose, no novels, just editorials,
doing penance for thirty years, never writing,
never writing you: eating, breathing, doing.
It's not like I didn't think of you.
I used to wonder, hear stories, a mother, a father, left their child,
never turned back. Now it was me, this a part of my autobiography?

After my father died (Thank God that competition's over!),
took a job, real job, management, ten years, did well, too, real man.
I stowed you away, locked suitcase in an attic, pictures of us together,
glass frames, some cracked though wrapped in heavy plastic.
I sometimes looked. I was afraid to cut myself.

Friends said why don't you contact him, call, a letter,
you know where he lives, and the years, decades rolled on,
and maybe I'd give it a whisper, like when the fall museum,
concert catalogues came out,
and I'd say maybe I'll get a subscription, take a pottery class,
Renaissance Art, but in a week, ten days, I'd throw them away,
knowing I couldn't dial your number.
I sent checks, heard stories; you seemed to be doing well.

I guess I wished you'd make the first move.
I'm the guilty one, sure, faithless, frightened, what if you didn't answer,
better to keep the cards in my hand, than take two, three new ones,
hearing my mother's high-pitched gin-rummy laugh as she knocked with four,
her lipsticked Philip Morris in a cut-glass ashtray near by.

And then last fall something came towards me, warily,
like a journeyman club fighter, six-rounder, old St. Nicholas Arena,
his sweat mingling with mine, feinting with his left,
hitting me hard with his right, the old brawler,
Death himself, we both waiting in our neutral corners
for the judges and referee's unanimous decision.

But this time the child didn't ask, wasn't a child anymore.
He come up out of nowhere, saying,
'Aleph, Bet, we could start again, not from the beginning,
but we could start. Look, your voice hasn't changed'.

Confessed he, too, all these years, afraid to speak, secreted, smothered,
'steadily more naked, but disguised by wearing clothes.'

And that neither of us could know the end of our next poem.

---

[1] Dr. Philip Bromberg died on May 18, 2020. He was a renowned psychoanalyst and author of many groundbreaking articles and books. The poem's title and next to last line come from a lecture he presented at the Division 39 (Psychoanalysis) Spring Meeting in New York City on April 28, 2017.

**Why I Believe in Ghosts**

When I dream I see my father
just home from the winter store,
taking off his gray long-johns
behind the French bedroom doors,
mother at the stove,
rib steak, bone-in.
He comes to the table,
knocks down two, three shots of Chivas,
saying, 'regular poison,' (shakes
his head furiously), smiles at us,
still chilled, hungry.

And when I wake I think he's still alive,
still there, 6'1", 200 pounds,
and it takes me time (I need to shake myself as well)
to return to the present, next to my new wife,
my father vanished.

Haven't I walked down Broadway in daylight,
seen someone who's dead, someone who's passed,
walk by me going the other way, the same gait, the same eyes,
a woman who taught in the room next to mine for thirty years,
or a man I knew from Nyack, only person who ever told me
he was afraid to drive across bridges.
At the curb I stop, turn,
too late, they're down the block. I never follow them.

My wife wishes her simple wish:
Once a year her parents could return,
maybe on their wedding day, birthday.
It doesn't sound impossible to her,
not asking for much.

When we decided to marry we visited
our parents' graves,
hilly Mt. Moriah across the bridge in Jersey,
New Montefiore off a Long Island highway,
no March wind, straggly grass, a few pebbles,
Hebrew letters etched into the heavy tablets.
We bend down, voices low to the ground,
introducing one another to our folks.
All four of them are silent.

We think of ghosts appearing behind us,
sneaking up, and never think of the hard work
the perfected dead, their remnant bodies, must do,
shoveling through crusted earth to reach us.
And what if all ghosts were body, once and forever?

I must believe in ghosts because I soon will be one,
never losing my taste for egg rolls, red wine,
your long legs (the first thing I noticed about you),
roughing my hands through your hair in bed.

And I must believe in ghosts for my children, both in their 50's.
I write these poems for them.
Paper, pen, and ink are real.

And I try to convince myself that it's all right to leave
my poems, incomplete, unpublished, cut off,
like at the end of last year when the doctors sliced
into me, attaching parts of bone,
and I asked myself, 'Who is me?'

And I think of my mother from Warsaw, the Bronx,
shouting at my father in the used white Cadillac
the morning they leave the city for good:
'Leo, you're taking me out to Long Island to die!'
And she tells me, her 'handsome son':
'It goes by so fast." And funny, the week after
my father died, I drove the Caddie right through
a red light, not thinking, my mother in the
passenger seat. The officer let us off.

## Half Sestina on my Mother's Centenary

When I was born, say it was my first lifetime,
I was taken from my mother's arms
if I was ever there at first, taken,
with warm nurse's hands, placed in a metal box.
Glass never enters my imagining, cold, grey iron,
four pounds two ounces, tubes, oxygen a question.

What my mother thought, felt, I never questioned.
She, twenty-three, immigrant from Warsaw, lifeline
with her first-born cut, staring at the iron
box, maybe there *was* glass to see through, her arms
helpless, bereft, frightened to touch the tiny box.
Did she cry, Bella, did you cry, too late to say.

It was your first lifetime let us say.
So stunned I had no questions.
Fifty years later, another metal box
on wheels, another severed lifeline.
I didn't take you in my arms.
I kissed your forehead smooth as iron

'Mama, why so cold?' my whispered question.
White sheet separates our very first lifetime
together and apart.

**Coupons**

There's a story I've never told anyone.
I've told some stories about my father's dying.
His long stomach cancer. He died August 28, 1989.

But not this one.

This was a few weeks after I went with him
to the oncologist in a small plain office in
Smithtown. He was receiving chemotherapy.
He asked the doctor, 'Do I have a year?'
The doctor answered (this was June):
'You won't make it 'til Thanksgiving.'

My father,
right-handed home-run hitter
in the early Sunday morning games
with other fathers in the Catskills,
now 73, riddled with what
would take him from us,
heard this like I did.

He told me once when I visited:
'I might look OK from the outside,
but it's inside. I'm sick inside!'

Words have power. Don't you know?
Words have power!
This strong man began to cry.

Words hit me:
Straight sledge hammer.

But that's not the story I've never told.

And it's not the story a few weeks after he died,
me and my mother alone
in their one-bedroom attached condo
near the Smithtown Mall.
You could count on your fingers, maybe one hand,
the times we've been really alone, fifty years,
without sisters, children, without my father,
and it is after dinner, dishes done,
still light in the September sky,
sitting next to one another on the
couch, touching hands, and my mother says to me,
'I never needed you before.'
We watch 'Dumbo' in color together on TV.

Now the story I've never told:

My father reads an article about China in the 'Times.'
'Why am I reading this? I will be dead soon.'
He hands my mother a bunch of food coupons
before we go out to the Cadillac
for the short drive to King Kullen.
I drive though the car seems much too big for me.
My mother never learns to drive.

My father keeps coupons in a small wooden box with a lid.
Categories: dairy, produce, paper.
He cuts them out carefully from the local Long Island weekly.
Rectangles. No margins. 15 cents off, buy two get one free.
This week only.

The supermarket is large, bright, many aisles.
My mother tears the shopping list in half,
written in my father's perfect,
old-fashioned Bronx public-school hand.
We share six coupons between us.

I complete my list.
Happy to find all my sale items.
When your father is dying
any small thing a son can do.

I walk one aisle, another.
Keep looking.
In the middle of an aisle stacked high
with canned vegetables, metal cart half-full,
my mother, bent over, coupons in one hand,
crying.

'I can't find them all,' she says.

## Company Fruit

Potatoes would make it home OK. Onions, too.
Nothing you could do to them.
Simpson lettuce, cukes, apples from Upstate,
Half watermelons, small black pits.
Fragility didn't matter here.
Durable like my father's two hands.

Sure we sold really good stuff in boxes slanted on the sidewalk stands:
Bing cherries, big, 10 Row, Washington State,
dark dark red, you would say purple. Bunches of grapes,
smooth ovals, pale green, sweet summer corn.

What else my father brought home each night:
Banged up peaches from an overfilled balsa basket,
small, brown dents in them, skin shredding in places,
California plums, too ripe to sell, Santa Rosa's, Italian 'L's.
Cantaloupes bruised right from their rectangular wired wooden boxes,
a dime a pound cheaper than the larger ones, perfect,
kept separate in a fat bushel inside.

Banged up, not good enough, but after Mom took her small black
kitchen knife, and cut away the flesh that was rotten,
she cooked what fruit remained,
simmering slowly, swirling in a pot, then cooled, and put in the
Frigidaire.
'Compote,' she called it as she served it for dessert
to my father, my little sisters, and myself.

It's not like we never set out beautiful, fragrant fruit
in the living room or on the foyer telephone table.
It was only that we children learned not to touch, taste,
put out only on Sundays with a name
we repeated and never forgot: 'company fruit'.

And you should know that after fifty years,
held imperishable,
I refuse to wash clean my soiled fruit store hands,
but I learn, I learn, to pluck Sunday grapes,
bring them to my mouth.

**Compound Words**

When I was a little boy
in the Bronx
World War II just over
my mother
pushing  a big high
carriage with
my baby sister in it
walked into a bakery
and the woman
behind
the counter
gave me
in my out-stretched
hand
the last small
oval
of seeded rye
from the slicer.
I walked out
mouth full
holding
my mother's
free hand.

Mom left Warsaw
1929
never left New York
never finished
10th grade
three children
all school teachers
six grandchildren

One late afternoon
1970 Queens Blvd
I come for dinner
mom back and
forth
kitchen
to the  TV
potatoes
boiling
Bird's Eye peas
Dad not home yet
6:30 news
her nose
six inches
from the screen
and
she's yelling
at Nixon,
she's
yelling,
yelling:
'Anti-Semiten
Anti-Semiten'

**I Wish My Father Had Told Me**

I wish my father had told me just once I was good
enough. Now it is too late. But I keep talking

to him, almost thirty years in a simple box in the
Long Island ground. My hair white as his was,

bald spot if I could look down, I know Dad's
photo exists somewhere, probably in an album
in my sister's closet, high school graduation,
first in his class, 1932, deep black hair, parted

exactly in the middle, he never went further,
and what I need to ask, but was afraid to ask,

when I had the chance, when I had the chance,
surely he loved me, called me, 'Number One Son,'

what I need to ask you Leo, father, yes, my fault
I never did, look at me, I'm not talking about love,

I'm just asking, just once: Can you ever, will you *bless*
who I was, still am?

## 'I am doing things I haven't done before.'

> Esa-Pekka Salonen from a New York Times interview
> about his newly composed Cello Concerto.

I am sitting in Philharmonic Hall, Second Tier Center.
Bought the last ticket up there.
Binoculars around my neck.

Not easy to get them focused,
shoot far above the stage.
I need to bring them down to scan the whole orchestra,
not ready, willing, to stay with
the young conductor, the harpist in the corner,
percussionist in the back, the world-famous soloist.
I want the breadth, the panorama.

And with my cane resting between the seats,
I go back sixty years, winters and summers,
to my father's fruit store, Buhre Avenue below the 'El,'
sawdust on the floor, green wooden stands
with wheels outside, bushels, boxes replenished,
a fullness, and twelve hours a day,
the big Emerson on a shelf above the cash register,
WQXR, only fragments as we rush, father and son,
outside for two pounds of wet spinach,
inside to weigh three pounds of potatoes
on the shaking metal scale.
Beethoven, Debussy, Verdi, taken in, osmosis,
as I write figures with a pencil on the side of the bag
adding and carrying over numbers for the total.

Now through my binoculars,
I am looking at the rows of violins, precision bows,
copies of themselves, like infinite mirrors,
and then at Yo Yo Ma, and I notice him
turn the page, at one with the conductor,
playing notes all up and down his cello, shrieking sounds,
something giving birth, and I see his gray hairs,
and I think that he and all the violins
know we are all dying, but play, play,
'Furioso,' as if they've just discovered fire.

**Perilous: June 1986**

I've walked six long blocks from my home in Hastings.
I could meet anyone I know, I've lived here
14 years, someone could wave to me as I
pass the Gulf station, OK, but why am I walking
to the grassy cut-out at the entrance to the Saw Mill?

Where's my mind? I'm 46, married 25 years,
and my legs are shaking. There I am, there
I am, 2pm, waiting for the rusted Volkswagen,
dirty wool blanket covering the pulled-down
back seat, thinking how we pushed aside
the kids' car seats, tangled straps, freeing
enough room for us to lie there.

I know I'm a perfect fool.
Standing there by myself, short-sleeved shirt,
I'm thinking of a Georgia O' Keefe painting
I saw once in a book. Painted white ladder
leaning on nothing. Blue sky.
I never forgot its title:
'I Want, I Want.'

## Nyack, N.Y. Winter Morning 1988

I never bought a TV. I'm sure other people do.
People in my position. My wife and
daughters in the house across the Hudson.
Me in an old Victorian studio, Main Street,
porch outside, you can see in,
antique car showroom across the street,
black Rolls in its big plate-glass window.

I am smoking Pall Malls now for four months.
When I wake in the Jennifer convertible
I tell myself out loud to the high ceiling,
the fireplace roof that doesn't work, its netting
torn, bird shit fallen in the grate, I tell myself:
'Up and at 'em, go get 'm.' I dress fast,
light up, go across the street for hot coffee,
egg on a roll, leather coat zipped, collar up, gloves.
I eat at the card table my mother gave me when
I told her I was leaving my marriage.
She gave me old dishes, silverware, taught me how
to put on pillow cases inside out. My '82 Riviera,
parked outside. I hope it will start today,
warm it up, ugly smoke sputtering.

My girlfriend has gone back to her husband, children.
When she left two months ago,
I could barely breathe, took the Buick
to her house, hiding, saw her buckle her children
into the Infinity, waited 'til they disappeared,
then drove home across the Tappan Zee,
glad, so glad, to have so many red lights
in the blurry cars in front of me
guide me home.

## Silent Watchman

I'm shopping with my father in Smithtown.
He makes three, four stops:
I am 47, in the passenger seat. And I'm going crazy.
Crazy about a woman. But I don't know I'm going crazy.
I only know I've got to reach her, 35, beautiful,
she told me she misses her young children.
Gone back to them, her house on the Sound.

A year before his cancer is diagnosed. Maybe he had it already.

I jump out of the car at every stop. Swing shut the heavy door.
I rush to a phone booth, dial the number:
long rings, no answer.
Each time, I get back in the car, wait for my father,
hear him click open the trunk, unload his purchases,
get back in the driver's seat.
But I don't think of him, never think of him,
don't think how he's feeling helpless, 70 years old.
Where's the son he knew? Professor, husband, father.

We don't say a word going home.

The winter before in Florida, married to my mother 50 years,
he tells me he'll give me $3000 to pay my kids' college loans
if I go back to my wife.

I never chased 'Nookie,' he says.
I refuse his offer.

Thirty years before, I had a summer job with the
Silent Watchman Company.
I had to open small locks at the bottom of Bronx store front doors,
replace thin sheets of narrow paper with
markings recording when the door opened or closed.
Break-ins, late openings, early closings.

Normally I would walk it, bus it.
But when he could, my dad would drive me.
It cut the hours in half, same pay.
And we could talk. When we got home,
he'd build high lunch sandwiches for us both,
cut them carefully in half.
Maybe have a beer together. He'd say, 'Beer belongs!'

The winter before he died, I never visited him in Florida.
He complained of pain in his stomach. Six months after his operation.
I didn't pick up his Sunday morning calls.
Let the phone ring. Never flew down. Alone, angry at myself,
my parents,
angry at the woman who said before we made love,
'You're fogging up my glasses!'

That April at my sister's house in Rockland,
I watched as dad got out of the driver's seat.
Holding my mother's arm, he was paper thin, bald, bent, shrunken.

I've never forgiven myself for not going down.

## Mt. Sinai New York: December 2016

I

Halfway more than halfway
less than halfway leaning both ways
back and forth, but the shaded window is far away,
and I hold on to the plastic buzzer to call the nurse,
my lifeline, and I have given up lifting the lid
on the oval food tray, my sheets in disarray,
naked beneath my stained blue gown, and
it is nine pm and the curtain can't protect me
from the patient's light across the room.


II

And when you have left gone home
paper bag half-eaten Danish, warm
orange juice on the windowsill, and,
yes, when you have wrapped your long
winter scarf around your neck,
it's not only too many hours 'til daylight,
a fool's errand to blank the mind,
in the hallway beyond my hearing now, nurse's laughter,
rolling BP carts, telephone's repeated rings,
and I hear a voice, not God's,
God does not appear in any form,
just a voice, soft, almost soundless, saying,
'Look, it's been enough, Genuch!,'
and I think of my mother, dead of a stroke
alone in her apartment, her black dress hanging over a chair,
New Year's Day, 1990, about to see 'Phantom of the Opera,'
a small smear of fading reddish blood on her mouth
when I find her lying in the gray hospital morgue.

We are by ourselves.

And my father four months earlier
in a morphine haze telling me
he won't have to drive Christmas trees from Upstate in the snow,
and he has seen his mother Fanny and his sister Sylvie waiting for him,
and on his last day, lifting himself up from his bed at North Shore,
telling me, his only son, 'it's working!'

III

I got what my father taught me: black and white early talkies' actors,
no names above the title: Brophy, Pangborn, Blore, cabby, hotel clerk,
butler.
I got shyster lawyer Dombrille, Guy Kibbee, Alan Jenkins,
all gone before me.
I got Jimmy Gleason throwing in the towel at ringside,
tears in his Irish eyes.
Demarest, waving a half-chomped cigar, saying, 'Come on Kid,
it's nothin',
we all done it easy, slide down the chute!'
Remember Jack Oakie, hoofer with the wide mouth, inviting Shirley
Temple:
'Baby, Take a Bow!' So now he says to me, 'it's your turn,'
I'm the one asked to take a bow, and I'm halfway, more than halfway,
leaning that way, and at least I'll have company,
guys I can count on, guys who work on contract,
better than being here alone,
only ten-fifteen, nothing I can do to make it later.

IV

I'd been haunted for thirty years by the title of a book I'd never read:
'Death Comes for the Archbishop,' and I think of Walter,
my portly financial advisor, who came to the house twenty-years ago,
big leather briefcase, spread papers on the dining room table.

I would sign some, and he would say, delicately:
'If you should depart the scene,'
and my daughters rush to the hospital from Vermont, from Baltimore,
walk me around the ward, see right before their eyes
the line I remember from 'Lear':
'There goes my father poorly led,' and they bring books and sweets,
and leave with a certificate from the One-Day University of Endings,
and though it's only like the old out-of-town tryouts in Boston or Philly,
for them it's plenty.

I am so glad to see them, that they have come, talking of nothing,
doing the Sunday Times crossword, asking me for words,
any words. 'How many letters?' I ask from my bed.
'Five and the middle letter is an R.'


V

And almost midnight I count my breaths one to ten and over again,
and from a huge height look down on my body in a long metal box,
and am not surprised, 'inevitable,' I say, and pull myself back, and
the next thing I know it's five am, a miracle,
and the man with a hospital nametag who tugs at me, asks:
'Can I take your blood?' and I ask him,
'Do I have any left?' and we smile, and, jabbed by this stranger,
I am grateful I am not alone, and it is almost morning.


VI

And then, 'Lux Erat!' Light Was, and I buzz the nurse.
I want the sheets and blankets straightened. I want a clean new gown.
I want to go to LA and see the palm trees,
a few palm trees, green and brown,
swaying in the December sun along some West Hollywood street,

nothing fancy, block with auto repair, old record store, Jack in the Box,
or wait in line for barbecue chicken, special sauce, paper plates,
across from the Ferris wheel in Santa Monica.

And many years ago in a borrowed Dodge,
I drove way up Mulholland Drive and saw lemons hanging from the trees,
and drove back, stop and go, shirtless along Route 1.

VII

And three hours later before you take off your coat,
you bring hot coffee from the outside and an apple turnover,
fresh, fresh, and I see in your worn, beautiful face:
'I can do this, I *must* do this,' your determination telling me,
'No, it is not enough, not 'Genuch!'

## I Don't Give a Damn about Revision

'I don't give a damn about revision!'
Just came out of me. I'm lying in a narrow
hospital bed at Mt. Sinai, wires, beeps,
bolstered toilet seat, blood clots in my lungs.
77, lying there; don't tell me there's no Angel of Death.
He's on the ceiling; he doesn't have to speak.
We are in contact like when my cell phone pings, think it's a friend,
it's Verizon Wireless, bill two months overdue. $465.

Make it to morning, Nurse Theresa, smiling, wheels me to the shower,
leaves me with a wrapped bar of harsh soap, towels,
new blue gown outside. Naked, I can't see the scar on my back,
but make up my mind then and there:
'You got to stop with the regrets!' What?
Didn't see Bobby Short at the Carlyle?
Never went to Ebbets Field? Failed marriage?
Never smoked marijuana, scared, uptight, my kids so young;
didn't take them to Europe; didn't get in a plane 'til 35,
bare feet finally touching the Pacific at Redondo Beach.

Made up for it in spades.
Premier Cru in a cave with 60,000 bottles in Beaune;
Grand Canal at dawn, men loading their goods from the shore;
black and white calligraphy in the Shanghai Museum's cool spacious
rooms.

All after 65 with my third wife, Judy, a miraculous late diving catch,
like the one Willie Mays caught over his head
in the glove (it is said) where 'triples go to die.'
I told her on an LIRR train months after we met:
'If it wasn't for you, I would have died unfulfilled.'

So when I said, 'I don't give a damn about revision,'
it isn't that I don't tinker with a word here or there,
move around stanzas, play with line breaks.
I might even use a dictionary.

It's that this morning, at our beach house,
a small swallow, a baby, cracked against the bedroom window,
sharp, brief, and I saw its tiny body on its back,
not moving, under an outdoor metal chair,
and I didn't want to open the screen door
with an old broom and dust pan, a paper bag,
and have it accidentally touch my hand.
I didn't want to touch its death, and waited.
And as I looked it seemed to have turned over,
and at the sound of the door screeching,
waved its little wings and flew off into the green trees.

## I'm Waiting for the Poem to Write Itself

I'm waiting for the poem to write itself.
Peter says it can happen that way.

Red volcanic burst, boiling, leaving no fingerprints, or
like Apple Sauce, the kitten who walked through our open screen door.

If I call, it doesn't answer. I call again.
God said, 'Evening,' and 'Morning.' And pronounced it 'Good.'

I notice half-lines, lines people say to me, or I say to myself,
and it occurs to me that some way back I left an unfinished sentence.

Friday morning before school mother sends me to the Kosher butcher
for a fresh, cut-up chicken wrapped in smooth brown paper.

And what just happened? Certain as the unfaded Chinese writing
inside the door of our antique wine cabinet,
I take the pen in my left hand.

I transcribe what is given.

## Found and Made Poem

It is 6pm.
I get on the downtown #1train at 96th Street.
I'm one away from an old man, soft flapping hat, open
crumpled raincoat, thin brown cane between his legs.
He's talking mid-stream, talking to the people opposite,
talking to himself.

Turns to me, our eyes meet, and I'm ready to listen
because I'm very anxious about the CAT scan
they're doing 7pm on my kidneys.
He's talking loud, but not shouting. Speaks slowly.
Says he writes the addresses and phone numbers
of new people in pencil, on a piece of paper,
not on an I-Phone, not on a computer.
He's definite about this, and I tell him
I'm the same way, have a small address book,
pages coming apart, that I never throw out.
He says, Yes, but people die, or you don't see them for years,
you might knock on their door, they're not there,
they've moved. But they might be there,
and maybe you could have coffee with them some time.

He says You're married 30 years, right?
I nod, lie, and he tells me about his sister and
her fiancé, says the man loved his sister so much,
came to ask her father's permission to marry,
and the father says, 'You love her you say, but do you like her?'
Like more important, he says. Like is much better.
His sister's divorced many years.

He tells me at weddings women throw bouquets.
Do I know what men throw?
I shake my head.
They throw their 'little black books.'
They don't need them anymore.
All the men jump to catch them.

The train stops at 72nd Street.
People are smiling at us.
He turns to the passengers, says,
You think I'm crazed. I'm not crazed.
I write the addresses and numbers down in pencil.

He tells me he sees we're both old, says he's 76.
I'm 79, I tell him. I say I've been lucky so far.
He says, No, not lucky, blessed.

At 42nd Street, I tell him it's 42nd Street.
He jumps up with his cane,
crosses to the open doors, says:
There'll be two people will remember you.
God and me.

## 'One more song he had'

> *'One more song he had*
> *and now the song is gone for good,*
> *gone for good.'*     Hayam Nahman Bialik

It would be a surprise to me any day it came,
because I'm so used to being here,
making my coffee, Times at the door,
my wife still sleeping, grown daughters safe.

I'm trying to write a poem, this poem,
here in our West End building where
two women died last week, 85 and 86,
one discovered by the doorman,
two days' newspapers outside her door.

I'd like it to be here, home, in my old plaid bathrobe,
new pajamas my wife just bought me at Century 21,
not all wired and beeping, kind nurses from
how many countries, women and men,
wiping my behind clean, my sprayed urine,
putting new blue gowns on me how many fucking times.

I'd like to be awake:
And the night before, brushing my wife's shoulders,
her sweet breasts, with my long fingers, and afterwards
wanting desperately to see Wendy Hiller and Roger Livesey
climb a hill on the Isle of Mull in the 1945,
'I Know Where I'm Going.'

## Still Life

I had the thought last week that death was working inside me.
That it was inside, softly working me. Pale ivory watercolor.
Every poem I write now is a late poem.

Like Cezanne's last apples, pears on a table,
I don't care what anyone thinks. Put away doubt.
I had the thought last week that death was working inside me.

My daughter Genese buys fine small pens, tiny Italian notebooks.
She walks hand-in-hand with Stephen, a new aphorism on his lips.
Every poem I write now is a late poem.

We walk the November night, my arm lightly around Peter.
He is going away. We sing together, 'Strangers in the Night.'
I had the thought last week that death was working inside me.

I translate 'Still Life' into French without hesitation.
'Nature Morte.' You could hear a pin drop.
Every poem I write now is a late poem.

Self-portrait and still life are the same.
What I came to say: my retraced blue jar, cylinder of remaining wine.
I had the thought last week that death was working inside me.
Every poem I write now is a late poem.

## If I Can't be an Angel

*If I Can't be an Angel What I Really Want is to Plant
an American Flag in the Ash of Some New Planet*

My cardiologist points to the screen. My birth date: 6/20/39.
'Yes, you're normal, OK? The date alone, that's why you're being tested.'

From my old, worn dictionary, I discover that
angels are the lowest of the nine celestial orders,
below Seraphim, Principalities, Archangels.

But if I were accepted, I would not complain.

How much room is there for error?
I like to think that I would slip in.
Don't we all think we are owed some special dispensation?
No matter what, don't I always make my bed, wash my hands,
get dressed, put my desk in order. Sometimes I even wear a tie.

I left two wives, the second fifteen years ago,
the first for another woman.
Like Isaiah who told the Angel, 'I am a man of unclean lips.'
Does teaching 7,000 students in the Bronx for 35 years
wash clean the afternoons I slowly drove away?

I remember when my father ran out of luck.
Buried with a triangular folded American flag.
There's another one up in my bedroom closet.
I don't know how it got there.
Maybe we forgot to follow his final instructions.
He told them to us, me and my sisters, hunched around his bed.

## Mephistos

I bought a pair of soft suede, lilac-colored shoes, with white soles.
$400, my first Mephistos, only made in France the salesman said.
Told me they would last 8,10 years,
company would replace soles, heels for a lifetime.

They're still in their box.
I have ten days to exchange them.
I'd never paid more than $200, always brown or black.

When my mother's father died, they covered the mirrors with sheets.
My mother gave me my grandfather's new shoes.
Why waste a good pair of shoes?
I never wore them. They scared me.

My father told and retold
how his immigrant mother, my grandma Fanny,
threw out his baseball spikes, dirty, black,
lying on their sides all winter in the back of the foyer closet.
The story always ended: 'You can't wear them in the house.
You can't wear them in the street!'

I remember walking my daughters
across Queens Boulevard,
the youngest in a stroller,
to the small shoe store next to the German deli, old movie theater.
They would try on little leather shoes with straps across the ankles,
get free balloons, rides on the painted mechanical horse outside,
wanting more.

Today
I heard a hundred children shrieking in the September schoolyard.
Running, jumping, climbing. So many of them spread across the yard.
I saw them through a silver chain-link fence.

I didn't want to leave them. I don't want to leave this world.

I'll keep the damn shoes.
Lace them up.
Wear them outside tomorrow.

Neil Grill initiated this collection three years ago in a Central Synagogue poetry class directed by the poet Jessica Greenbaum. He continues as a member of the 92nd Street Y Himan Brown Senior Center poetry workshop, directed by Frances Richey. All the poems in the collection have been written in the past three years, under the supportive aegis of Fran and the excellent poets and friends in the 92Y group.

Neil teaches poetry writing in Fair Harbor, L.I.

Neil was a professor of English for 36 years at Bronx Community College (CUNY). A Ph.D. in English from New York University (1971), he was also Department Chair for seven years in the 1990's. After his retirement, he returned to school and received his MSW from the Fordham Graduate School of Social Service, and a certificate from the ICP (Institute of Contemporary Psychotherapy) Four-Year Psychotherapy Training Program. He is a NYS Licensed Clinical Social Worker (LCSW).

In his thirties and forties, Neil published about 40 poems in various poetry journals and magazines. He did not write another poem for 30 years, devoting himself to teaching, departmental administration, and, later, social work education and analytic training and practice.

Neil is married, has two daughters, and two grandchildren in their twenties. Brought up in the Bronx, he currently lives with his wife, Judy Smith, in Manhattan.

www.ingramcontent.com/pod-product-compliance
Lightning Source LLC
LaVergne TN
LVHW041505070426
835507LV00012B/1336